MW00875008

Gary Jones

Venice

First published by Gary Jones in 2016.

Copyright © Gary Jones, 2016.

All rights reserved. No part of this publication may be reproduced, stored, or transmitted in any form or by any means, electronic, mechanical, photocopying, recording, scanning, or otherwise without written permission from the publisher. It is illegal to copy this book, post it to a website, or distribute it by any others means without permission.

This book was professionally typeset on Reedsy.
Find out more at reedsy.com

Contents

1

Introduction

Venice must be one of the most enchanting cities in the world.If you are traveling to Italy and you don't visit Venice, then you missed out on the biggest treasure in Europe.

Many travelers have limited time to visit a city like Venice and often feel overwhelmed by the amount of choice that a city like Venice has to offer.Unfortunately, these travelers miss out on the best of Venice.With this in mind I wrote this travel guide.

Don't make the mistake that many travelers make. These travelers have 2 or 3 days in the city, and they try to see everything and end up being overwhelmed and exhausted. They actually start missing home.

There is a better way to do things. Take the best Venice has to offer and make that your focus. This will give you a short but amazing experience.

This guide will show you the best Venice has to offer and will give you a unique perspective of this amazing city. This guide will make 3 days feel like a week. When the planning is done for you, everything feels easy .

This guide will give you all the information you need to make your short stay in Venice one of the most memorable times of your life.

Have a great time in Venice

Good Luck!

2

Understanding The Modern Venice

The city of Venice, as described by William Shakespeare in his 1596 and 1598 play, The Merchant of Venice was undoubtedly a booming city with lots of wealthy businessmen and an organized trade.

The city's strategic location in the middle ages and Renaissance period coupled with the Venetian's hard work is what bore the magnificent houses, castles and palaces that the city had before its fall started in the 13th century when Venice tried to hold Thessalonica unsuccessfully from the Ottoman's in 1423-1430.

Venice also fought a 30-year war with the Sultan Mehmet II after which it started losing its competitive edge over other empires in Europe. The Black Death also struck in 1348, 1575 and 1577 leaving a third of the population dead.

Another blow to Venice's economic might was when it lost its place as the center of international trade in Europe to Portugal. A visit to the city will reveal the remains of what was once the economic powerhouse in its time; splendid landmarks, waterways, bridges, the people, the alleys, canals and the piazzas spell what remains of the city's magnificence at the height of its might.

The monumental buildings that are paved with canals represent what were once palatial residences for some of the famous nobilities at the height of Venice's economic boom.

The modern Venice as it stands represents a wealth of architectural treasures and splendid works of art that the Venetians were known for. One of the outstanding characteristics of Venice that make it a must-visit city for many is the fact that it is surrounded by water from all the sides. When you go to Venice, you won't find so many streets as in most conventional cities around the world; instead, you will find canals just beside the narrow passageways that pedestrians walk on.

This magical floating city in the Northern end of the Adriatic Sea and North of Italy boasts of being one of the 118 small-submerged islands that are grouped together into an archipelago that features over 400 footbridges that move across 177 boat canals that connect the city making it easy to move around. The bridges are often arched to let traditional boats (commonly referred to as gondolas) to pass beneath.

The whole of Venice including its lagoon has been listed as a World Heritage Site. Its splendor coupled with its majestic beauty explains why it receives an average of 50,000 visitors daily making it one of the 30 most visited cities in the world accounting for international arrivals going well over 25 million visitors.

Do you know that some of the world's most renowned personalities have their homage in Venice? For instance, Marco Polo, the great explorer, and Antonio Vivaldi, the great musical composer hailed from this magnificent city where streets are replaced with shimmering canal waters.

Venice has also been famously described as the city of Casanova thanks to the great playwright and lover, Giacomo Casanova who lived in the 18th Century. William Shakespeare in his famous 1597 play, Romeo and Juliet, described Venice as the city where Othello married Desmoneda, the Venetian. Images of love as depicted in Romeo and Juliet and those of hate as depicted in The Merchant of Venice and lots of other creative works of art come into mind when most people think of Venice.

The city is one big maze that you will get lost in, not once but serially. However, the most intriguing thing about it is that each new street you come across will be worth the hassle of knowing your way around because it is rich in beautiful bridges, waterways and splendid architecture of churches and palaces that will leave you breathless. Actually, as you get caught in the many winding and seemingly endless bridges and streets of astronomical confusion, walking will be your only solution. However, you soon discover that the city is one big maze of breathtaking adventure that will make you explore it even more as you try to find your way around; every turn will reveal something that will make you forget about the trouble you been going through to find your way around.

From tiny cobbled courtyards to arched bridges, winding back streets, obligatory gift shops, traditional tratorrias (restaurants) and osterias (bars), every turn you take in the city will usher you into a breathtaking view of the scenic waterways such that you will be spoilt for choice on which places you should take a photo of.

In a city where the number of tourists accounts for a significant proportion of the city's population, you probably wouldn't want to be walking in the already crowded walkways along the pathways in the city center. Instead, you can break away from the many tourists that flock the Piazza San Marco then head towards the narrowest alleyways where you will experience the utter description of romance by simply being there. The maze created by the alleyways is worth having a map if you want to find your way around with greater ease.

3

How Venice Came Into Being

Although there is not much detailed information on how the city of Venice as we know it came into being, the available evidence and some tradition have pointed historians to March 25th 421AD, on the day that is famously known as Saint Marks's Day.

Actually, the original population of Venice constituted refugees from different Roman cities near the region such as Altino, Treviso, Padua and Doncordia who were fleeing from Hun and Germanic invasions. This was after a Byzantine Duke moved his patriarchal seat to the place where Rialto stands today.

The refugees, who were originally farmers constructed their houses on the marshy lagoons after which they started fishing and conducting salt trade. That's when these people were later on referred to as lagoon dwellers or incolae lacunae since they lived in the lagoon. At the time, the city's strategic location gave these farmers a competitive edge and even molded the Venetians to become sailors.

Later on, the growing city was granted city trading rights along the Adriatic coast. The city withstood many of the wars that occurred in its early years making it to emerge as the super power of the Mediterranean region at the height of its power.

At the time of its formation, Torcello was the most important village in the lagoon; that's why they built the Cathedral there in 639 AD to act as a refuge for those escaping from the barbarian invasions. The Venetians built the footbridges to connect several islands within the lagoon.

The city's Doge's government was established in 726 AD after which the construction of the Doge's palace (Palazzo Ducale) started in 814AD; this is the present day St. Mark's Square. The construction of the Basilica St. Marks started in 834 the original basilica burned down.

Venice spread out quickly to such places as the Adriatic sea then took part in Crusades that were meant to free Jerusalem. Due to its strategic position, Venice benefited a lot from these wars. For instance, such items like the four bronze horses of St. Mark's (now found in St. Mark's Museum were some of the loots.

Marco Polo, the Venetian merchant moved from Venice to China in 1271-1275; in his journey, he met Gengis Khan. This is probably one of the most fascinating true stories of the Middle Ages.

Fast forward to the period between the 9th century and the 12th century when Venice experienced astronomical growth and developed into a city while maintaining its strategic position in commercial and naval power. During this period, the city flourished as the main trading center between Western Europe and the other parts of the world; this was a period of boom for the Venetians. This however didn't last forever; in 1348, the plague struck leaving almost half of the population dead.

Majority of the people living in Venice at the time were rich and powerful. It was during the Fourth Crusade when it became apparent that Venice was the sea superpower of the Mediterranean Sea. Just to get on the same page here, Crusades simply refer to military campaigns that were instigated by the Latin Roman Catholic Church to fight against the Islamic powers. These were long-running religious wars at the frontiers of Europe. In the Fourth Crusade, Venice stood out as the preferred trading and war-staging hub in the Adriatic Sea as it traded with the Muslim World and the Byzantine Empire.

During this period, Venice grew to become the leader of the four sea powers of the Mediterranean Sea ahead of the Republics of La Spezia, Genoa and Amalfi. Later on, in 1489, Venice conquered the island of

Cyprus.

Even with the booming economy and lots of rich and powerful people, the poor also lived among these people; that's why the world's first Ghetto was founded in 1516. This went on for close to two centuries until another plague struck in 1630 leaving a large proportion of the population dead. This meant that the city became more vulnerable to attacks and in 1797, the city fell into the hands of Napoleon Bonaparte making it part of the Hapsburg Empire (currently Austria). Under his rule, the city took a new direction as a hub for marvelous literature, architecture and art. Actually, Bonaparte was somehow seen as a liberator among the Jewish population when he removed the gates of the Ghetto, effectively ending the restrictions that controlled the way Jews lived and traveled in Venice.

The Venetians revolted between 1848 and 1849 resulting to the reestablishment of Venetian Republic under the rule of Daniele Manin. This didn't last long though since Manin's rule was overtaken in 1866 after the Third Italian War on Independence effectively making it part of the newly created Kingdom of Italy.

The famous Giacomo Casanova, as depicted in the book 'Memorie di Giacomo Casanova', was born in 1725.

Fast forward to 1902 when the refurbished Modern Art Gallery opened its doors at Ca' Pesaro as part of inheritance from Bevilacqua-La Masa, the Duchess and the collapse of St. Mark's square bell tower; you can buy photos of the events that unfolded that day when you visit Venice. The modern bell tower was re-built completely in 1912 to make it as it is today.

As you will notice when you visit Venice, one of the most famous places to visit is the Palazzo del Cinema, which opened its doors at the Lido di Venezia; the original size was later enlarged in 1952.

During the time of World War II (1940-1945), the city went on untouched except for Operation Bowler, which never really destroyed anything of historical value. This doesn't mean everything stands as it was back in the day. Actually, 16000 homes were destroyed in 1966 by floods when water level reached 2 meters; you will find many of the old churches with marks showing where the water reached on the November 4th 1966 flood. In 1996, a fire struck at Teatro La Fenice destroying everything; this was later re-oppened in 2004 after years of reconstruction.

How Were The Magnificent Structures Made?

When you visit Venice, you might probably wonder how the early Venetians managed to built houses almost in the water as marked by the canals that mark the streets in the region. You will marvel at the architectural wonders including basilicas, castles, grand palaces or palazzos; how did they come into being given the probably crude construction methods they used at the time?

To start with, the magnificent ancient buildings that spell the city's years of boom were constructed on larch pylons, which refer to closely spaced wooden piles that were submerged under the waters; these have stood the test of time even after years of submersion. So, in simple terms, the foundations of the city lay on these closely spaced wooden piles. The piles were made from trunks of the highly water resistant alder trees. Since water is low in oxygen, these trees, which are already water resistant decay at an astonishingly slow rate. The Venetians later on added slabs of Istrian stone, which is similar to marble but much stronger to make the foundations stronger as they penetrated a layer of sand and mud until they reached a much harder layer comprising of compressed clay.

The construction process wasn't easy and was time-consuming. For instance, one of the popular churches needed up to 1,106,657 piles of 11.2 feet long each to construct; it took over 2 years to get this done. The Venetians didn't have much of an option but to build on the water since the land wasn't strong enough to hold the buildings. So, in essence, the city was built this way not because the people wanted it but due to utter necessity.

With its rich history and spectacular sceneries, Venice is definitely a must visit destination for most of us. Perhaps I should remind you that the city is slowly sinking so Venice as we know it won't be as it is in the next few centuries. Even if you won't be alive by then, you probably wouldn't want to go down the history lane without having known one of the world's most spectacular places.

4

An Overview Of The City

Venice has been arranged into 6 sestieri/districts or sixths since the 12th century; the Grand Canal (which you will probably see on your visit to Venice) divides the city into two with three sestieri on each side of the bank.

On the farthest end is the **Lido(11-kilometre long sandbar in Venice**), while the central district is known as **San Marco**; this one is characterized by the Rialto Bridge and the Grand Basilica di San Marco. The area is also characterized by some high end five star hotels, high-end expensive shops and tourist trinkets just to mention a few; if you visit Venice on any day, you will probably find more tourists around this region.

Another district, **Castello**, lies right beside San Marco and contains a host of first class hotels as it stretches towards the east where the hotels and restaurants are not so expensive, a region called Arsenale. The **Arsenale** region constitutes one of the key locations for the international art Biennale.

Cannaregio occupies the area that is north of the train station. At least a third of the population in Venice lives in this area; you will also find the cheapest restaurants and hotels in this region.

To the Northwest of Rialto lies **San Polo**, where one of the most famous churches, Santa Maria Dei Frari is built. Scuola di San Rocco, which has some of the most renowned Tintorento paintings, is also in this region.

Santa Croce is the least visited region of Venice just across the train station to the north of San Polo district. This doesn't mean that there is nothing to attract people there; in fact, you will be amazed by its rich history of architecture and art. The district's center is Campo San Giacoma dell-Orio even as it stretches up to the Piazzale Roma area.

For nightlife, the city's number one district of nightlife is Campo Santa Margherita square in Dorsoduro, which houses numerous late night bars and restaurants. This region isn't just about nightlife; you will find the famous Peggy Guggenheim and Accademia galleries and the Punta Della Dogana. The district also boasts of the La Guidecca, which is located within a short vaporerro ride from Piazza San Marco just across the Grand Canal. The famous Capriani hotel is also located in this region.

Just for your information, a vast majority of travel around the Venice is by canals. Actually, there are no roads for cars in most of the places in Venice since people use canals and waterbuses while others walk. In fact, cycling is illegal in most of the regions in Venice. However, if you would still want to use vehicles or ride a bicycle, you would need to head to the **Lido di Venezia** region, which has sandy beaches and countless resort star hotels that can give you a break from the city crowds.

Venice doesn't just end with the six districts; it goes far beyond to include the islands of Torcello, Burano and Murano. Torcello is famous for its magnificent Basilica of Santa Maria Assunta, which dates back to the Byzantine times. Burano is famous for lace making while Burano is known for being a glass-making center.

The best time to visit Venice

Now that you have decided that you want to visit Venice, what next? Timing is very crucial if you want to get the most from your visit. So, what is the best time to visit?

To start with, the period between spring and autumn, which is between April and October marks the peak season for tourists. The peak is also experienced over the Christmas season and during famous Carnival held in February. So, if you don't like crowds, try visiting another time such as during winter (the period between December and February (excluding Christmas)); accommodation is often cheaper during these times. You can also visit in the period between April and May as the high season is usually just picking up. Unless you like crowds, visiting during Easter, Christmas, The International Film Festival (held in August) and in February during the Carnival, should be out of the question.

5

Transport and Safety

You need to know how to get around if you don't want to spend your few days stay wandering in the streets not knowing how to move around; the clock is ticking so you have to get the most out of every minute. You can opt to book a hotel before travel or opt to hop around the city looking for your preferred hotels on arrival.

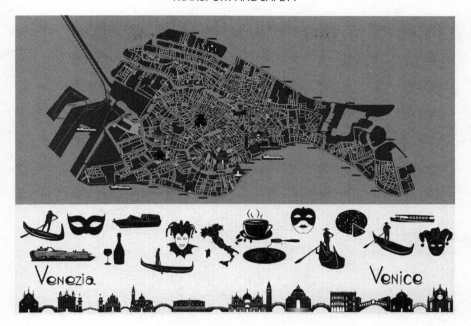

Assuming that you have landed at Marco Polo Airport, which is 7KM north of the city, where do you go from there? To answer your concerns, you need to order public transport tickets from the main reseller, Hello Venezia. You can choose to order the tickets online or buy them at the airport. You will find travel to destinations on the mainland and to the city just outside ground level of the arrival halls. You can use either of the following routes from the airport.

Marco Polo Website
http://www.veniceairport.it/en/
Telephone: +39 041 2606111
Marco Polo Airport Map
https://goo.gl/maps/FdrP3KGRmnv

Transport

1. Land Route
You can opt to use either of the following modes of transport:

Buses

You can choose to use ATVO direct coaches or ACTV local bus service Number 5 to take you to Piazzale Roma, which is 20-25 minutes drive away based on the traffic. Piazzale Roma marks the end of the historic, which is separated by water so you have to use ACTV waterbuses to move around the city.

Taxis

Any taxi outside the airport can take you wherever you want to go. The taxis should cost anywhere around €20 for the 15-20 minutes drive. However, ensure that you agree on the price before boarding the taxi.

Train

If you love adventure, you can opt to travel to Venice from London by train in just a day's ride. This service is provided by the Italian domestic train, TGV and Eurostar and will take you about 15 hours. Start by taking Eurostar from London to Paris (you should arrive by mid-morning) then board the high speed TGV (these depart 3 times daily) heading to Milan after which you can board Eurostar Italian Train to Venice Santa Lucia from Milan Centrale (this should take about 2 hours and 35 minutes. If you don't want to use the high speed train, you can board any of the regional Milan to Venice trains that should take about 3 hours 30 minutes. If you are on a budget, the Eurostar Italian train service should be the best bet since it is fairly reliable and affordable. You can book the Eurostar Italia and the Italian regional trains as early as 3 months from your expected travel time.

Italia Rail Website
https://www.italiarail.com/italian-high-speed-trains
Telephone: 1-877-375-7245
Email: info@italiarail.com

2. Use Private Water taxi

If you have heavy luggage, you can hire a private water taxi to take you to your hotel; you can book this when you arrive. When you hire the private water taxi, the charge caters for four passengers. Just for your information, all water taxis in Venice are metered so the charge is fairly fixed between € 80 – 120 depending on where you are going.

<u>Water Taxi Website</u>

http://www.venicelink.com/?option=com_content&view=front-page&Itemid=43&lang=english

Telephone: +39 041 240 1715

Fax: +39 041 241 716

How to move around

The best way to move around the city is on foot. The city is largely congested and has most sections where cars and bicycles are not allowed. The streets don't have roads but are replaced with canals so the only other option would be to move using boats. However, you should expect to be hopping on and off the water transport system to move to different places.

Walking will help you unravel the city's narrow and winding alleys referred to as Calle or Calli; these cross numerous small squares that are paved with small shops & souvenir shops that sell glasses, belts and lots of other goods.

The public transport system in Venice is very efficient; it is run by ACTV. It comprises waterbuses (vaporetto boats) that come in different sizes, which run on a fixed schedule. You could use connecting lines if you are traveling to different outlying districts like Guidecca, Burano, Lido, Torcello and Murano. These trips are also available at night.

Bikes

Bicycles and scooters are not allowed in Venice. However, you can rent one on the lido (Lido on Bike) between March and October; this shop is at 21 Viale Santa Maria Elisabetta, which is a few meters away from the main Vaporreto station. You can also call (041) 526 8019. Gardin Anna Valli is another spot you can rent a bike just on the same street. Call (041) 276 0005 for more details.

Traghetti

These are the ferries in Venice and they use the Grand Canal route crossing the Venetian waterways at 7 points between St. Mark's Basin and the railroad station. They are also referred to as Traghetto and form the main mode of transport for moving people across the different islands. These are much cheaper than the gondolas. However, they don't have chairs or luxury trimmings. Boats are quite many in this region so you shouldn't expect to wait for too long if you want to cross over to the other side of the city. A quick look at any street map of Venice will reveal straight lines that cross the Grand Canal and some yellow lines that point towards where the traghetto dock. The journey isn't too long so you can just stand (almost everyone will be standing).

The gondolas/Venetian boats

The primary mode of transport in Venice is water, as the city's streets are mainly canals. The traditional means of transport here is the Venetian boats or the gondolas, which are handcrafted by various traditional Venetian craftsmen who make them from eight different types of wood; the city only has 400 licensed gondoliers. A quick glance at the gondolas might reveal something symmetrical but the truth is that their left side is a little taller than the right side by 9.4 inches. Their shape and sections represent the six districts in Venice.

Taxis will have a black registration number displayed on a yellow background and can be found at Lido, San Marco, Rialto and Piazzale Roma among other places.

Venezia Unica City Pass

The Venezia Unica City Pass is perfect for organizing your visit to Venice, allowing you to access to public transport.You can plan your stay in Venice and get your tickets for transfers, the water-buses, museums, churches and much more.This is the best travel resource in Venice and recommend that you visit their website to find out more.

Venezia Unica City Pass Website

http://www.veneziaunica.it/

Safety

The city of Venice can look and feel fairly creepy especially during the night. However, this shouldn't be a cause for alarm. Cases of violent crime in the city are quite rare so you can walk around this magnificent city without much fear of being raped, mugged or murdered. However, this doesn't mean that the city of free of crime; nonviolent crime is also common, just like in many tourist cities around the world. For instance, camera thieves, pickpockets and purse lifters are plenty so be on the lookout. Here are some safety tips to help you stay safe:

1. Keep most of your cash, ATM, spare credit card and passport in a neck wallet or any other safe place. As a rule of thumb, don't keep money, passport or wallet in the hip pocket as it attracts thieves. Keep all valuables somewhere where people (thieves) cannot see. Don't tempt thieves!

2. Beware of hip packs and backpacks as someone can easily unzip them without you noticing especially in crowded places; they can steal anything valuable you have in there. Most of the popular places are filled with people; this includes such places like the Campanile di Marco and the Rialto Bridge. Ensure that you keep watch over your stuff to avoid pickpockets.

3. Don't tempt thieves by dangling your expensive stuff where thieves can see.

4. Keep in mind that Venice doesn't have a central lost and found office so if you lose something, that might be the end of it unless you are just lucky. However, if you lose anything on a train, you can visit the train's offices to inquire whether your item was found. Other places where you can check any lost and found item can be found here; you will also find other useful addresses on that site.

5. Be on the lookout for warnings of high tides (aqua alta) to avoid being caught up in a fix especially when you are around the Piazza San Marco where the tides could be quite high. You can tell the height based on the number of sounds made by the siren and the duration that each sound takes. Also, watch out for sudden storms that could quickly increase the water levels. Put on high shoes or boots especially during rainy or winter days, as most of the places will be flooded. Click here for more information.

6. Venice is highly infested with mosquitoes especially between July and October so you might want to carry a repellent.

Call the police if you feel you are in any threatening situation by dialing 112. If you have a medical emergency that does not need an ambulance, Ospedale SS. Giovanne e Paolo should be the best place to start. When you get to Campo SS. Giovanni e Paolo, follow the Ospedale signs that are north of the Piazza San Marco just close to the Fondamente Nove. The emergency entrance is just next to Ospedale waterbus stop.

Emergency Numbers

- Ambulance – 118
- Accidents and breakdowns – 116
- Fire – 115
- General SOS – 113
- Medical Emergencies – 118
- Police – 112
- Traffic Police – +041 274 7070

Now that you know how to move around Venice and how to stay safe during your travel, let us discuss some popular places you shouldn't miss out during your trip to this historical city. As I mentioned earlier, the entire city and its lagoon have been listed as a world heritage site so you could easily be spoilt for choice on where to visit.

As someone visiting Venice for just 3 days, you wouldn't want to start wishing to go back home because of engaging in so much such that you end up tired and cursing your trip. For the best experience, you need to have specific places where you would want to visit and what you want to do during your 3-day trip. Such places include visiting museums and art galleries, going for boat rides, sampling the city's cuisine and nightlife and doing lots of other things. Let's dive straight to it.

6

Hotels

Let's take a look at some great budget hotels for your stay in Venice:
- **<u>Domus Orsoni</u>**

This lovely bed and breakfast hotel is located in the Sestiere di Cannaregio.The Domus Orsoni has a fantastic atmosphere and the famous Orsoni family legacy can be seen everywhere is this unique hotel.This hotel has everything you need for your short stay, including a private safe and air conditioning.

Address: Cannaregio, 1045, 30121 Venezia, Italy

Phone:+39 041 275 9538

Domus Orsoni Website

http://www.domusorsoni.it/english/chisiamo.html

Domus Orsoni Map

https://goo.gl/maps/bTBTCSRxxok

- **Ponte Chiodo**

You can find this classic Hotel at the end of a bridge.It's located in an amazing area of Venice and just a 3-minute walk to the fantastic Ca' D'Oro Palace.This is not a modern hotel, but it makes up for it in character.If you want to experience romantic Venice, then get a room at Ponte Chiodo.

Address: Cannaregio 3749, 30121 Venezia, Italy

Phone:+39 041 241 3935

Ponte Chiodo Website

http://www.pontechiodo.it/en/index.asp

Ponte Chiodo Map

https://goo.gl/maps/1fmRCkE9F9s

- **B&B Sandra**

If you are looking for a nice and cosy bed and breakfast hotel, then B&B Sandra is the hotel for you.One of the main attractions in this hotel is the nice traditional Venetian roof top terrace.You will have fantastic views over the city and have one of the best breakfasts in the city.

Address: Corte Trapolin, 2452, 30121 VE, Italy

Phone:+39 041 720957

B&B Sandra Website

http://www.bbalessandra.com/

B&B Sandra Map

https://goo.gl/maps/t8WNr1a9xdk
· **Residenza de l'Osmarin**

This hotel is located in the heart of Venice and is very close to the Piazza San Marco.This hotel has a classic Venetian style and has fantastic service.The rooms are big, and most rooms have a nice view over the city.

Address: Castello, 4960, Venezia, Italy

Phone:+39 347 450 1440

Residenza de l'Osmarin Website

http://www.residenzadelosmarin.com/about-us/

Residenza de l'Osmarin Map

https://goo.gl/maps/6Z29zHfM7PP2

7

Museums and Art Galleries

Although Venice is in itself a museum owing to its rich history, a visit to the museums will reveal much more than what you see on the outside.

Here are some of the museums you can visit. Each Museum here links to its Google Maps page to help you get there with ease.

· **The Academia Museum**

If you want to learn more about 14th -18th-century art and paintings, you shouldn't fail to visit the Academia Museum. It is located just right ahead of the Academia Bridge and is open from Monday through Sunday. Opening times are 9.00AM-2.00PM on Mondays and 8.15AM-7.15PM from Tuesday-Sunday.

Charges are 6.5 Euros for adults and 3.25 Euros for EU citizens aged between 18 and 25. Kids aged 18 and below and those older than 65 receive free admission if you are an EU citizen. Call +39 041 522 22 47 for more details.

Website
http://www.gallerieaccademia.org/the-museum/?lang=en
The Academia Museum Map
https://goo.gl/maps/mqqwxLbSNYS2

· **Archeological Museum**

This features Babylonian, Roman, Greek and Egyptian antiquities and is open Monday-Sunday from 8.15AM-7.15PM. The museum is closed on December 25th and January 1st. An entry card costs 12 Euros; this gives you access to Correr Museum, Palazzo Ducale and Biblioteca nazionale Marciana. You can call +39 041 522 59 78 for more information.

Website
https://www.facebook.com/Museo-Archeologico
-Nazionale-di-Venezia-327299674024201/
Archeological Museum Map
https://goo.gl/maps/2eKZttkeRHE2

· **Oriental Art Museum**

This features porcelains and armors from the Edo times; features mainly Japanese art collection. The entry to this is through Ca' Pesaro Museum and is open from April-October, Tuesday-Sunday starting from 10.00AM-5.00PM. Charges are 5.5 Euros for Adults, 3 Euros for EU citizens of 18-25 years and free for those younger than 18 and older than 65 and are EU citizens. Call +39 041 524 11 73 for more information.

Website
http://www.arteorientale.org/sito/
ing_museo.html
Oriental Art Museum Map
https://goo.gl/maps/YgeBXPajRaN2

· **Marciana Library Museum**

This one is located right in front of the Ducal Palace and on the other side of the Piazzetta. Jacopo Sansovino built this magnificent structure in the 16th century. Palladio described it as the most magnificent palace ever built. To enter the museum, you should enter through the Napoleonic Wing of the Correr Museum.

This is open Monday-Sunday from April-October from 9.00AM-7.00PM and from Monday-Sunday from November-March from 9.00AM-5.00PM. It is closed on December 25th and January 1st.

Charges are 12 Euros for a Museum card, which gives you access to visit the Archeological Museum, Palazzo Ducale and the Correr Museum. Call +39 041 240 72 11 for more details.

Website

http://www.venice-museum.com/biblioteca-marciana.php

Marciana Library Museum Map

https://goo.gl/maps/XYEEfbNKCDB2

· **The Ducal Palace**

You must visit this former center of political power in Venice, which dates back from the 9th Century. When you visit, expect to see Sansovino's sculptures, government and law courts and lots of beautiful paintings including Veronese and Titian. Also, don't forget to visit Casanova prison cell.

It is open from Monday–Sunday starting 9.00AM–7.00PM from April–October and Monday–Sunday starting 9.00AM–5.00PM from November–March.

The museum is closed on December 25th and January 1st.

Charges are 12 Euros for a Museum card, which gives you access to Archeological Museum, Marciana Library and Correr Museum. Call +39 041 271 59 11 for more information.

Website

http://palazzoducale.visitmuve.it/en/home/

The Ducal Palace Map

https://goo.gl/maps/1mHsKXPsj1P2

· **The Correr Museum**

This was originally meant to be a dance hall but has since been converted to be a Museum for keeping Venetian History and Art. In here, you will find such things like Canova's sculptures, and lots of paintings dating back from the 14th -16th century.

Opening times from April–October are 9.00AM–7.00PM from Monday–Sunday while the opening times from November–March are 9.00AM-5.00PM from Monday-Sunday. The museum is closed on December 25th and January 1st.

Charges are 12 Euros for a Museum card, which gives you access to visit Archeological Museum, Marciana Library and Palazzo Ducale.

Call +39 041 240 52 11 for more information.

Website

http://correr.visitmuve.it/en/home/

The Correr Museum Map

https://goo.gl/maps/SjpArD9HbV32

· **Ca' Rezzonico Museum**

This museum comprises of furniture and works of art of the 18th Venetian century. The furniture and art is from the Seicento while the paintings come from, Giambattista Tiepolo, Canaletto, Pietro Longhi and Francesco Guardi.

Opening times from April-October are 10.00AM-6.00PM from Monday-Sunday while the opening times from November-March are 10.00AM-5.00PM from Monday-Sunday.

Charges are 6.5 Euros for Adults, 4.5 Euros for 18-25 year old EU citizens and 2.5 Euros for 18 years and younger and those older than 65 years.

Call +39 041 241 01 00 for more information.

Website

http://carezzonico.visitmuve.it/en/home/

Ca' Rezzonico Museum Map

https://goo.gl/maps/yBUr3570QZx

· **Ca' Pesaro Museum**

This museum has a number of other museums including Oriental Art Museum and the Modern Art Museum.

In this museum, you will find sculptures and paintings dating back from the XXth century such as Paul Klee, Henry Moore, Matisse, Chagall, Kandinsky, Klimt and Rodin.

Opening times from April–October are 10.00AM–6.00PM from Tuesday–Sunday while the opening times from November–March are 10.00AM–5.00PM from Tuesday–Sunday.

Charges are 5.5 Euros for Adults, 3 Euros for 18–25 year old EU citizens and free for 18 years and younger and those older than 65 years.

Call +39 041 524 06 95 for more details.

Website

http://capesaro.visitmuve.it/en/home/

Ca' Pesaro Museum Map

https://goo.gl/maps/qy5mEYPmyLm

· **Ca d'Oro (Golden House) Galleria Franchetti**

This features a wide range of collections dating back from the XVth century including Baron Franchetti's collection. You will also find paintings and Sculptures including those of Vivarini, Carpaccio, Tintoretto, Gorgione, Titian and Eyck among others. You will also find lots of bronzes in here.

This is open all year round Tuesday–Sunday from 8.15AM–7.15PM and on Mondays 8.15Am–2.00PM.

Charges are 5 Euros for Adults, 2.50 Euros for 18–25 year old EU citizens and free for 18 years and younger and those older than 65 years.

You can choose to buy a single ticket for 11 Euros, which also gives you access to Oriental Museum and Accademia. Rates for 18–25 year old EU citizens are 5.5 Euros.

Call +39 041 527 87 90 for more information.

Website

http://www.cadoro.org/?lang=en

Ca d'Oro Galleria Franchetti Map

https://goo.gl/maps/wKcZScKRBB72

Extra Time

Here is a list of other places and events to visit if you still have some energy left during your three-day visit.

- **Peggy Guggenheim Collection**

This Art Museum is located on the Grand Canal in the Dorsoduro Sestiere of Venice.The collection of art housed in the palace dates back to the 18th century.The American Heiress Peggy Guggenheim lived in this palace for three decades.Originally(1951) she occasionally displayed her private art collection to the public and after her death in 1979 she passed it to the Solomon Guggenheim Foundation.Today the gallery is open to the public every for most of the year.Art from major Italian futurists and American modernists can be seen at the gallery.

The museum is open daily between 10am and 6pm but closed on Tuesday's and December 25.Adults can enter the gallery for 15 euros and children are free.

Phone

+39 041 240 5411

Website

http://www.guggenheim-venice.it/inglese/default.html
Peggy Guggenheim Collection Map
https://goo.gl/maps/8V1xiTBa5CH2

- **Musica a Palazzo**

The Musica a Palazzo is an incredible experience for any visitor to Venice.The Musica a Palazzo is a cultural association of musicians who get together to produce opera performances that can be seen at the Palazzo Barbarigo Minotto.The Palazzo Barbarigo Minotto is a Venetian Gothic palace that is on the grand canal.The operas are performed with no stage wich makes it a spectacular experience with the crowd becoming part of the different scenes in the opera.The musicians at the Musica a Palazzo are world famous.

Phone
+39 340 971 7272
Website
http://www.musicapalazzo.com/language/en/
Musica a Palazzo Map
https://goo.gl/maps/ByWhCTMSpU52

- **Museo del Vetro**

The Museo del Vetro is a glass museum .The museum is located on the island of Murano, just of the northern coast of Venice.This museum is located in a Gothic style palace called the Palazzo Giustinian.The museum was founded in 1861 and has one of the most complete collections in the world.The work ranges from antiquity to the 20th century.

The Museum is open from Tuesday to Sunday from 2pm to 6pm.
Adults can enter for 3 euros and children for 2 euros
Phone
+39 041 739586
Website
http://museovetro.visitmuve.it/en/home/

Museo del Vetro Map
https://goo.gl/maps/XP1QpcMwH3m
· **Madonna dell'Orto Church**

The Madonna dell'Orto is a spectacular church located in the sestiere of Cannaregio.The church was erected by the religious order the "Humiliati".The church was built under the direction of Tiberion da Parma, who is buried under the church.In the beginning, the church was dedicated to St Christopher, but the popular name suggested that the dedication was to the Holy Virgin comes from the following century.Apparently the neglected statue was brought to the church from the nearby orchard.In 1399, a restoration project was financed by the city's Maggior Consiglio.The church was built on weak foundations, so restoration was critical.

The Church is open from Monday –Friday from 10am to 5pm.On Holidays, it is open from noon to 5pm.

Entry to the church is free, but the church asks for a donation to help fund the maintenance of the church.

Phone
+39 041 719933
Website
http://www.madonnadellorto.org/eng/index.php
Madonna dell'Orto Church Map
https://goo.gl/maps/XVWx4AVG2z82

8

Other Attractions

Squares

Venice is also rich in squares, which you should be on the lookout for when walking around the city. Squares are also called Piazza, Campielli or Campi and are mainly found in front of churches. You will notice Venetians simply love meeting and playing in these paved places. When you notice a Campi, you should probably also find a coffee shop around! Some famous squares include San Stefano and Santa Margherita since these are fairly bigger.

Bell Towers

Venice is rich in numerous bell towers that are in many cases adorned with the statues of gargoyles. You will find these in probably all the churches. The most famous tower, which is also the highest is the Bell Tower of San Marco Plazza, which is 98 meters high. It looks almost new since it was rebuilt in 1912 after it collapsed in 1902.

You could also visit Saint Mark's Bell Tower just to get an aerial view of Venice. Another popular bell tower is that of San Giorgio di Maggiore, which is located on the other side of St. Mark's basin. Just for you to know, Galileo introduced his telescope on the Bell tower of St. Mark so you might want to check it out (costs are 6 Euros) at the entrance.

If you are visiting the bell tower of St. Mark, please note that they don't accept visitors one hour before closing time so you must get there early.

Visiting hours:

April-June: 9.00AM-7.00PM

July-August: 9.00AM-9.00PM

September-October: 9.00Am-7.00PM

November-March: 9.30AM-4.15PM

If you come with a group of 20 people, you will pay 3 Euros per person unlike the 6 euros per person that is charged normally.

Saint Mark's Bell Tower Map

https://goo.gl/maps/kPeJgR1PVu82

· **Palaces of Venice**

The city's over 200 palaces are a representation of its diversity through-out its vast history as a maritime powerhouse of the Mediterranean region. Here are some of palaces to visit during your visit.

- **Palazzo Flangini**

This unfinished palace dates back to the 17th century. Guiseppe Sardi is the architect responsible for its majestic design and the Longhena architecture.This palace overlooks the Grand Canal .The entries to the palace are completely independent with exclusive docs.The palace is located in Campo San Geremia.

Address: Campo San Geremia, 252, 30121 Sestiere Cannareggio, Venezia VE, Italy

Phone:+39 333 707 1763

Website

http://www.valorizzazioniculturali.com/en/

Palazzo Flangini Map

https://goo.gl/maps/7DpcKZu7ocw

- **Palazzo Labia**

This Venetian baroque style palace was constructed in early 18th century by Andrea Cominelli and Allessandro Tremignon.The palace is unusual because it has formal front on the Grand Canal but also a formal facade at the rear.The side on the Cannaregio Canal is also decorated.This type of design is very unusual in Venice.Occasionally the ballroom of the Labia is used for international conferences.

Address: Campo San Geremia, 30124 Venezia, Italy

Palazzo Labia Map

https://goo.gl/maps/uoy9eN4E5er

- **Doges Palace**

You should also visit the doge's palace or the Palazzo Ducale, which is rich in history. Each room has something that speaks volumes about the Venetian's political administration during its height as a powerful maritime power and as a war staging zone during the middle ages and renaissance. This magnificent work of art was built by Bartolomeo

Bon and Giovani. It is open daily 8.30AM-7.00PM (closed at 5.30PM in winter). Call (0039) 041-2715-911 for more information.

Address: San Marco, 1, 30124 Venezia, Italy

Doges Palace Map

https://goo.gl/maps/KhStccbCNYu

Bridges

Venice boasts of over 400 bridges that connect palaces, gondolas and churches in this small city that have a characteristic arch and steps. Many of these bridges date back from the XIVth century although some modifications have been made to make them stronger and to prevent accidents. Only one bridge does not have the parapets (structures for preventing people from falling off the water) and this is the Bridge of Chiodo in the district of Cannaregio. Popular bridges include the bridge of Sighs and Bridge of Rialto just to mention a few.

· Bridge of Sighs

The bridge of sighs was constructed in 1602 to connect the façade of the ducal palace with the prison that was established in 1589.The view from this bridge was the last that prisoners saw before they went to prison. Most people refer to it as the bridge of the sorrowful. It is also the only bridge that is fully covered. Casanova is known to have escaped this prison according to his tales in History of my life. This is probably a must see.

Bridge of Sighs Map

https://goo.gl/maps/s2iPeGLLcfp

· Rialto Bridge

This bridge is one of the 4 bridges that currently cross the Grand Canal; it was once the only way you could cross the Grand Canal on foot (for close to 300 years). It was constructed between 1588 and 1598 under the supervision of Antonio da Ponte. You will definitely want to visit this location to take a few pictures and just marvel at the beauty and the architectural skillfulness of the builders.

Rialto Bridge Map
https://goo.gl/maps/UeVNsg5LkEr

· **The Grand Canal**

The Grand Canal is the main waterway in Venice. It takes an S shape that splits the city into 2 with three districts on either side moving from St. Mark Basin on one side of the lagoon to another lagoon that is near Santa Lucia train station. It measures between 30-90 meters wide while its length is about 3800 meters. The average depth of the Grand Canal is 5 meters deep and is now lined with ancient palazzi , beautiful castles, mansions etc, all of which are now museums. Ride on a vaporetto just to enjoy the scenery.

The Grand Canal Map
https://goo.gl/maps/uCNg2SXYKLN2

· **St. Marks Basilica**

Churches are quite many in Venice all of which are characterized by bells. St. Marks Basilica is probably the most popular. Originally a Doge chapel, this spectacular masterpiece features Italian Byzantine architecture. It was converted to a cathedral in 1807 when it acted as the seat of the Patriarch of Venice. St. Mark's relics lie on the foundations of this building. A visit to this place will reveal lots of stuff that I cannot start explaining in words; the feeling is simply breathtaking. You will find a statue of one of the four Tetrarchs dating back to 1204. You will also find a statue of St. Mark's horses.

Address: San Marco, 328, Venezia, Italy

Website

http://www.basilicasanmarco.it/?lang=en

St. Marks Basilica Map

https://goo.gl/maps/Pri1FntWFkJ2

- **St. Mark's Square (Piazza San Marco)**

This place is probably among the most beautiful squares all over the world. Lying at the heart of Venice, the L-shaped Piazza is often known as the drawing board of Europe due to its rich history. The area features the Basilica on one end, the Campanile bell tower at the middle and the Doge's Palace just nearby. You can rest here if you are tired since this spectacular place has seats.

St. Mark's Square Map

https://goo.gl/maps/UX5SyFwnChN2

9

Restaurants, Bars, Clubs and Nightlife

Restaurants And Bars

Experience a wide variety of sea-foods prepared from fresh marine catch in any of the following restaurants in Venice. I have grouped them based on where they are located in the six districts. Each restaurant here links to its Google Maps page to help you get there with ease. You will probably find Italian wine and international wines in most of the restaurants.

Restaurants in Cannaregio
- **Fiaschetteria Toscana**

Has wonderful service and fairly conventional cooking so you shouldn't expect any surprises. Expect such stuff like light light tagliolini neri al ragu di astice referring to some thin black noodles that are served with some delicate lobster sauce. This one is located at Salizada S. Giovanni Grisostomo, 30121 Cannaregio, Venezia VE, Italy ; you can call 39 041 528 5281 for more information.

Website

http://www.fiaschetteriatoscana.it/

Fiaschetteria Toscana Map

https://goo.gl/maps/grFwL7A3CuS2

- **Dalla Marisa**

This is an excellent traditional Italian restaurant, and it has a great Italian family atmosphere.They usually have a set menu where you choose between meat and fish.They don't take credit cards so bring cash.

This one is located at Cannaregio, 652 30171 Venezia Italy. It is quite small and always full so book in advance by calling +39 041 72 11.

Dalla Marisa Map

https://goo.gl/maps/dY7Zj84Szxj

- **Vini da Gigio**

This has affordable prices and is fairly romantic. It is located at Sestiere Cannaregio, 3628a 30121 Venezia Italy. Call +39 041 528 51 40 for more information.

Website

http://www.vinidagigio.com/

Vini da Gigio Map

https://goo.gl/maps/3WKgPDPMSgS2

Restaurants in Castello
- ### Corte Sconta

It is best to reserve a table by calling +39 041 522 70 24 since this restaurant is often full. It is closed on Sundays and Mondays.

Address: Calle del Pestrin, 3886, 30122 Castello, Venezia VE, Italy

Website

http://www.cortescontavenezia.it/

Corte Sconta Map

https://goo.gl/maps/fe6LSQ6yRNp
- ### Enoteca la Mascareta

Eat some crostini and drink good grappa in this renowned bar and restaurant. You can call + 39 041 523 07 44 for more information. The restaurant is located at Calle Longa Santa Maria Formosa, 5183 – Castello.

Website

http://www.ostemaurolorenzon.com/

Enoteca la Mascareta Map

https://goo.gl/maps/JXNEwzTeSF72
- ### Alle Testiere

This one is one of the best in the area so you shouldn't expect any bad surprises. They are located at Calle del Mondo Novo, 5801 – Castello or you can call + 39 041 522 72 20 for reservations

Website

http://www.osterialletestiere.it/Testiere/Benvenuto.html

Alle Testiere Map

https://goo.gl/maps/ECwqGwTvu6x

Restaurants in Dorsoduro

- ### Angelo Raffaele

This one is fairly priced and has delicious food. You can call +39 041 523 74 56 for more information. The restaurant is located at Campo Anzolo Rafael, 1722 – Dorsoduro.

Angelo Raffaele Map
https://goo.gl/maps/xo1LxExYyzv

- ### Cantine del Vino "Già Schiavi"

This is one of the very best in the district even though it is fairly small. You can call +39 041 523 00 34 for reservations. The restaurant is located at Fondamenta Nani, 992 – Dorsoduro.

Website
http://www.cantinaschiavi.com/en/
Cantine del Vino Map
https://goo.gl/maps/PGKeNyFQcNG2

- ### Harry's Bar

This one is located at Calle Vallaresso, 1323 30124 Venezia Italy. This bar dates back to 1930s and is best known for its Bellini cocktails and carpaccio.

Website
http://www.harrysbarvenezia.com/
Harry's Bar Map
https://goo.gl/maps/5GC1gxpUGex

Restaurants in Santa Croce

- ### Pizzerie AeOche

This one is located at Calle del Tentor, 1552 – Santa Croce. You can call them at +39 041 524 11 61.

Website
http://www.okevenezia.com/en/

Pizzerie AeOche Map
https://goo.gl/maps/DukRG4DcMXC2
- **La Zucca**

This one is located at Ramo del Megio, 1762 – Santa Croce. You can call +39 041 524 15 70 for more information.
Website
http://www.lazucca.it/en/
La Zucca Map
https://goo.gl/maps/XiVZqLMzHLk

Restaurants in San Marco
- **Acqua Pazza**

This serves mainly Mediterranean-inspired seafood, pizza & pasta. It is located at Campo Sant'Angelo San Marco, 3808 Tufo LT, Italy
Website
http://www.veniceacquapazza.com/
Acqua Pazza Map
https://goo.gl/maps/NTXnuepRA6m

- **Bistrot De Venise**

This one is located at San Marco, 4685 30124 Calle dei Fabbri Venezia, Italy. It has some delicious cheeses, salami or prosciutto.
Website
http://www.bistrotdevenise.com/
Bistrot De Venise Map
https://goo.gl/maps/z84h5qJKzJT2
- **Al Colombo**

Located just near the Rialto Bridge at San Marco 4619 Venezia, Italy, this one will wow you with its great Italian wines and dishes. It has been

famous since the 1700s. You can call + 39 041 522 2627 for reservations.
Website
http://www.alcolombo.com/en/
Al Colombo Map
https://goo.gl/maps/a4cGDwbfuy72

Restaurants in San Polo
· **Trattoria alla Madonna**

This one is located a few steps from the Rialto Bridge and about 100Meters from the middle Calle Della Madonna at Calle de la Madona, 594 – San Polo. You can call +39 041 522 38 24 for reservations.
Website
http://www.ristoranteallamadonna.com/
Trattoria alla Madonna Map
https://goo.gl/maps/8YiyzvWV79u
· **Cantina Do Mori in Venice**

This one is located at Calle Ochialera, 429 San Polo. You can call +39 041 522 54 01 for more information. This is an old-school wine bar that do Tramezzini stuffed with cheese, veggies and meats.There are no tables, just a long wooden bar.Apparently Cassanova was a regular in this bar.Great old school experience.
Website
https://www.facebook.com/pages/Cantina-Do-Mori/129503543767439
Cantina Do Mori in Venice Map
https://goo.gl/maps/dUECjwyPmGo

· **All'Arco**

This is located at Calle dell Ochialer, 436 – San Polo, which is just adjacent to Cantina Do Mori. You can call +39 041 520 56 66 for more information; it is one of the very best around. It opens from midday.

This is a standing bar only and a great place to drink wine and enjoy bar a fusion bar menu with snacks like asparagus and courgette-flower rolls stuffed with ricotta and ham.Maybe you want to try something different like calf's liver with parsley and onion.This another unique Venice experience.

All'Arco Map
https://goo.gl/maps/Ji9LYoQWxn22

Nightlife-clubs

Even if some streets in Venice look almost deserted at night, you will find some nice spots to dance the night away. Here are some of the best night joints throughout the city.

- **Molocinque**

This is one of the best and features a color changing pool, enough space, several bars and nice furniture. There is lots of music in here so if you like techno, Latin dance music, 80s and 70s music, this is the place to be. It is located at Elettricità, 8 Marghera VE, Italy.

Website
http://www.molocinque.it/
Molocinque Map
https://goo.gl/maps/F37GRKrbUXP2

- **Bacaro Lounge**

This bar plays some nice music and is one of the liveliest spots in the city playing jazz music. It is located at San Marco, 1345 30124 Venezia Italy.

Website
http://www.bacarojazz.com/
Bacaro Lounge Map
https://goo.gl/maps/FhRhsQyJZT12

- **Margaret Duchamp**

This is one of the best nightspots to be, especially if you want to stay late at night. It is located at a relatively quiet neighborhood in Campo Santa Margherita, 3019 Venezia, Italy. It is open until 2am.

Website

https://www.facebook.com/Margaret-Duchamp-358773637545144/

Margaret Duchamp Map

https://goo.gl/maps/xaxvke7XoVm

10

Boat Rides in Venice

Boat rides in Venice

You cannot visit Venice and fail to take a boat ride whether you are moving from one side of the city to the other, or you simply want to experience the city from the many canals that replace the conventional roads in most cities.

Venice has an 117 small islands connected by canals and linked by bridges.So you will spend a lot of time on the water.Try out the different boats in Venice and explore the different canals and islands.

Your most memorable experiences will probably entail getting lost in the city, seeing Venice from above (bell towers) and from the water as you ride the various boats.

The top 5 Boat Rides in Venice

- **Ferry/ Traghetto**

This is a cheap way to experience the Grand Canal.When you get to an area where there is no bridge then just jump on the Traghetto and get across.This a cheap way to have fun and save time in Venice.

- **Topetta**

The Topetta is a traditional Venetian boat that can take 5-6 people.The Topetta is a great way to experience Venice with Friends.

Address: Calle Carmelitani, Venezia, Italy

Phone:+39 327 256 5008

Topetta Website

http://www.laltravenezia.it/en/costi.php

Map

https://goo.gl/maps/3WmgfacULk22

- **Dinner Cruise**

The Dinner Cruise is a great way to experience dinner in Venice with spectacular surroundings.Make sure you plan your trip perfectly because the dinner cruise is only on Wednesdays.

Tel. 39 0421.380006

Dinner Cruise Website

http://www.jollyroger.it/

- **Vaporetto or Public Boat**

These boats are the public transportation of Venice.Vaporetto is probably not the most relaxed experience in Venice but a cheap and easy way to get around the city.

Vaporetto or Public Boat Website
http://www.veneziaunica.it/

· **Burchiello Boats**

A long time ago Venice and Padua were connected by river boats.The river boats were called Burchielli.These days the Burchiello boats serve as long distance touring boats between Venice and Padua.The Burchiello boats are modern and comfortable.The cabin has sofas, air conditioning, bar and toilets.The deck on the boat offers the passengers amazing views.

Tel. +39 049 8760233
Burchiello Boats Website
http://www.ilburchiello.it/en/tour

11

Sample 3 Day Itinerary

It can be overwhelming to visit all these places and do everything that is there to be done in just 3 days. Failure to have a plan will probably make you end up wasting too much time in a single location or simply doing too much such that you end up not having the energy to see everything that the city has to offer. To make your three day stay less hectic and more practical, let me take you through a sample itinerary to ensure that you get the most from your short tour to Venice. If you don't have a guide, it is best to book your reservation online to skip the long queues that are often in many of the tourist locations where you have to pay.

- **Day 1:**

-Visit Doge's Palace and the Bridge of Sighs for 2 hours
-St. Mark's Square, Bell Tower and Basilica-3 hours
-Take pizza at Arca for late lunch
-Visit Galleria della'Accademia (this is about 15 minutes away from St. Mark's Square via Ferry #1
-Take dinner cruise on Galleon Dinner Cruise if it is on a Wednesday
-Sample Venice's nightlife by visiting Margaret Duchamp

- **Day 2**

-Visit Rialto Bridge and Rialto market (don't touch the fresh produce

here) for 1 hour

–Take note of Ponte della Paglia and San Giorgio Maggiore that is right across the lagoon

–Visit Peggy Guggenheim Collection for about 2 hours

–Take a vaporetto trip along the Grand Canal (watch out for the Santa Maria della Salute) along the Grand Canal.

–Take late lunch at Al Colombo

–Visit the academia bridge that crosses the Grand Canal and just gaze at the city

–Take dinner at Acqua Pazza

· **Day 3**

–Visit Ca' Rezzonico for about 2 hours

-Visit Isola di Burano for about 1 hour

-Visit Museo del Merletto for 2 hours

-Take lunch at Enoteca la Mascareta

-Visit any other place of your choice or do anything else you want to do

-Take dinner at Pizzerie AeOche

-Attend any of your preferred nightclubs in Venice

I recommend losing your map for once and just experience the maze that the city has to offer. Getting lost is part of everyone's memories of Venice; in any case, it is a small island, which you definitely cannot get lost in all your life! You can always ask for directions to St. Mark's Square so that you can retrace your footsteps!This guide have linked you with google maps,so if you get lost just get online and the map will guide you.

12

Conclusion

I want to thank you for reading this book ! I sincerely hope that you received value from it.I hope you now have a better idea of what this amazing city has to offer.

If you received value from this book, I want to ask you for a favour.Would you be kind enough to leave a review for this book on Amazon?

Check Out My Other Books!!
http://www.amazon.com/Budapest-Best-Short-Travel-Guides-ebook/dp/B013Z0EZ20
http://www.amazon.com/Amsterdam-Best-Short-Travel-Guides-ebook/dp/B010E2R9NY
http://www.amazon.com/Prague-Best-Short-Travel-Guides-ebook/dp/B015T8FZVG

Ó Copyright 2016 by Gary Jones – All rights reserved.
This document is geared towards providing exact and reliable information in regards to the topic and issue covered. The publication is sold with the idea that the publisher is not required to render accounting, officially permitted, or otherwise, qualified services. If advice is necessary, legal or professional, a practiced individual in the

profession should be ordered.

- From a Declaration of Principles which was accepted and approved equally by a Committee of the American Bar Association and a Committee of Publishers and Associations.

In no way is it legal to reproduce, duplicate, or transmit any part of this document in either electronic means or in printed format. Recording of this publication is strictly prohibited and any storage of this document is not allowed unless with written permission from the publisher. All rights reserved.

The information provided herein is stated to be truthful and consistent, in that any liability, in terms of inattention or otherwise, by any usage or abuse of any policies, processes, or directions contained within is the solitary and utter responsibility of the recipient reader. Under no circumstances will any legal responsibility or blame be held against the publisher for any reparation, damages, or monetary loss due to the information herein, either directly or indirectly.

Respective authors own all copyrights not held by the publisher.

The information herein is offered for informational purposes solely, and is universal as so. The presentation of the information is without contract or any type of guarantee assurance.

The trademarks that are used are without any consent, and the publication of the trademark is without permission or backing by the trademark owner. All trademarks and brands within this book are for clarifying purposes only and are the owned by the owners themselves, not affiliated with this document.

54529279R00037

Made in the USA
San Bernardino, CA
19 October 2017